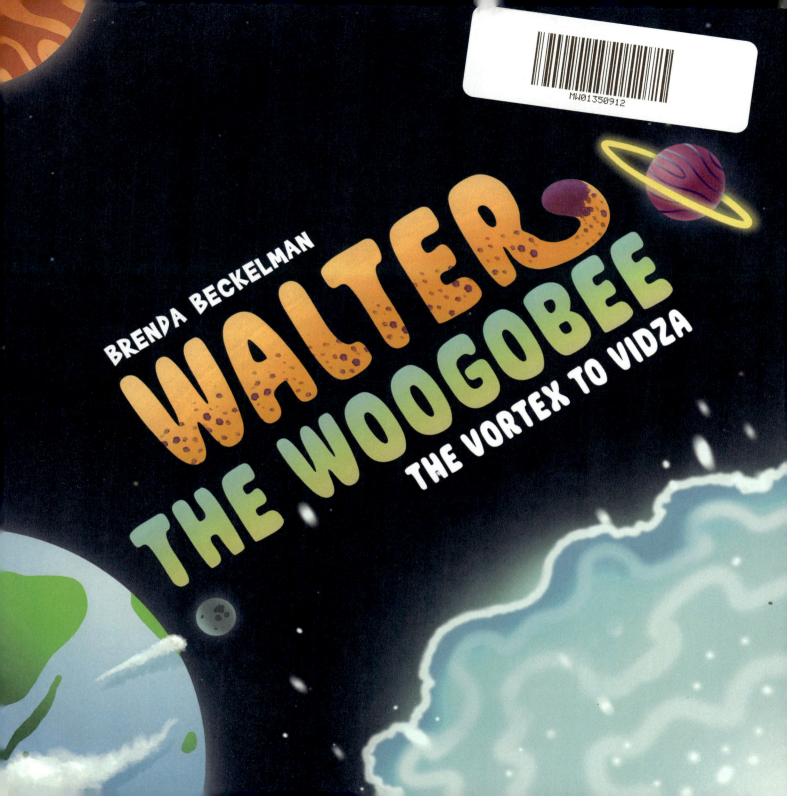

Copyright 2023 Brenda Beckelman

All Rights Reserved. No part of this publication may be reproduced, distributed, or transmitted in any form or by any means, including photoshopping, recording, or other electronic or mechanical methods without prior written permission of the author and publisher, except in the case of the brief quotations embodied in reviews and certain other noncommercial uses permitted by copyright law. For information regarding permission, email the author at WalterWoogobee@gmail.com

This book is a work of fiction. Names, characters, and incidents, are either the product of the author's imagination or are used fictitiously, and any resemblance to actual persons living or dead, business establishment, events, or locales, is entirely coincidental.

First Edition Book, September 2023

Book cover design, illustration, editing, and interior layout by: 1000 Storybooks

www.1000storybooks.com

DEDICATION

Dedicated to all of my kindred spirits in the world.
Enjoy the fun adventure.

Walter tumbles to the ground, not knowing where he is, and it is so hot! He sees creatures coming toward him. What are these strangers? Could they be lost pets? One is leaning over him. It speaks!

"Hi there little guy, are you hurt? Who do you belong to?"

Walter just stares at them, because he is so shocked that these pets can talk. It takes him a moment to respond.

"My name is Walter. I'm a Woogobee."

"A Woo-go-what? Wait, you can talk? Wow!"

"I'm Bayon. I live here; this is Arizona, but… how did you get here?"

"Our planet was being hit by an asteroid," Walter explains, "and my dad built this thing he calls a World Vortex Locator so I could find a new home. I pushed some buttons, but nothing happened. Then I ran outside and the next thing I know, I am here!"

"Wow, cool."

"Do you know how to use the Vortex Locator? Can you travel anywhere in the galaxy?"

"I don't know—I'm just a kid, and I'm not sure how everything works.."

They push a few buttons, then, suddenly, Bayon and Walter disappear!

"Walter, what happened to you?"

"I can change shapes for a short time and sometimes it happens when I get scared."

"Look! I see something hiding in the trees."

A girl comes out of the forest, carrying a sphere aimed at them.

"I can speak any language," Walter whispers to Bayan. "I'll tell her we're friendly and just lost."

She says her name is Kian and that they are in Vidzas. She is the village's pathfinder scout.

The wind howls loudly and Kian says it is not safe here—the Windmaker Monsters are heading this way.

They hurry to the village, just beyond the forest. It looks like a tornado hit. There are windmills everywhere, many of them destroyed.

Kian explains that their homes are all in the clouds; the windmills create air waves for the crops and the elephants use them to carry people to their houses. She explains that the village is being destroyed by the Windmaker Monsters.

"They have been attacking us and stealing our wind, creating storms, and damaging our windmills," she says.

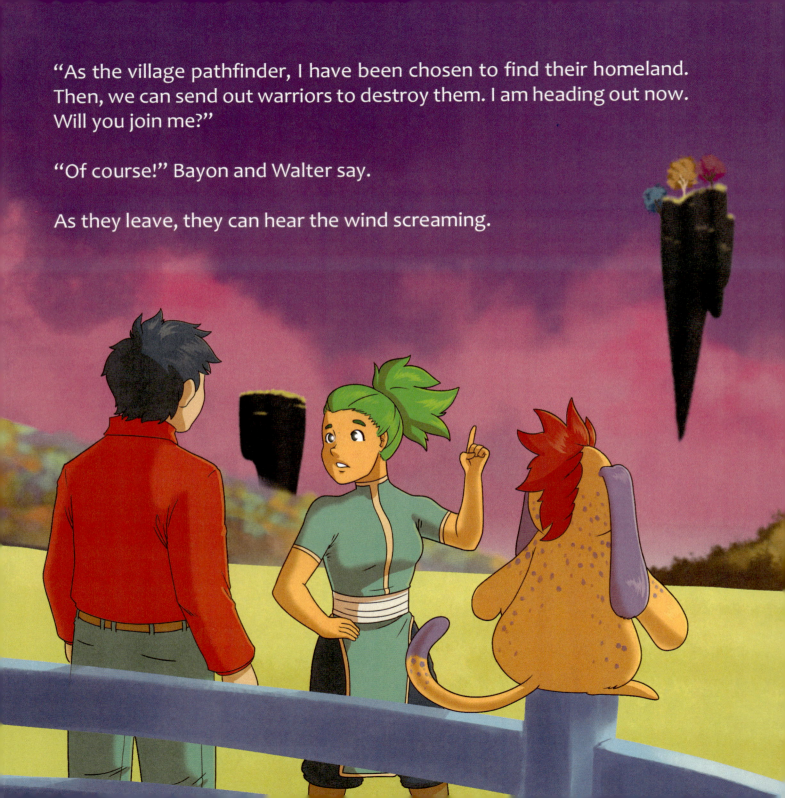

"As the village pathfinder, I have been chosen to find their homeland. Then, we can send out warriors to destroy them. I am heading out now. Will you join me?"

"Of course!" Bayon and Walter say.

As they leave, they can hear the wind screaming.

"Do we know where we are heading?" asks Walter.
Kian explains, "The elders have told tales about the Golden Valley and Wind Village over the mountains."

When they reach the base of the mountains, the air smells like rain, the wind stirs, the trees sway, and rain falls. Chilling sounds fill the air.

They hear a loud voice: "…Turn back…Go away…Beware…Do not enter the Golden Valley!"

They run quickly into the mountains…toward the Golden Valley and Village of the Wind!

The trek across the mountain is rocky with narrow trails. Upon reaching the top of the mountain, they can see the most beautiful valley below and what looks like pots of gold.

As they enter the Golden Valley, Kian discusses the folktales she has heard about this valley and the Leprolions that protect it.

"None in sight, so let's try to cross as fast as we can to the woods where the wind village is."

Suddenly a Leprolion jumps out, roars, and runs toward them! They run as fast as they can, but the big cat almost catches Bayon and scratches his arm.

He screams and Walter, who was ahead, turns to see Bayon almost get bitten. He quickly turns into a dragon and blows fire at the lion, singeing its fur. The lion turns and runs away.

Kian quickly gathers herbs for Bayon's wound and it heals instantly. They continue on, taking turns watching for the Leprolions and the Windmakers.

As they approach the wind village, they are captured in a wind trap. Wind is on all four sides of them, surrounding them with winds so strong they cannot move.

They hear the same loud voice: "…Why are you here?"

"Our friends from the Village of Vidza need your help. Please will you listen to us?" Bayon says.

The walls are removed and a giant funnel appears. "I am the WindMaster. The Vidza Village steals our breath of life, the wind. They hurt our people."

Kian starts to cry as she explains that they did not know this and are so sorry. "Your wind hurts my village by destroying our windmills, which we need for food."

Walter asks the WindMaster how the Villagers steal the wind.

"The Windmills redirect our currents. If the village will get rid of the windmills, we can provide them with natural wind in whatever direction they like."

Kian is so excited and happy. "That would be fantastic!"

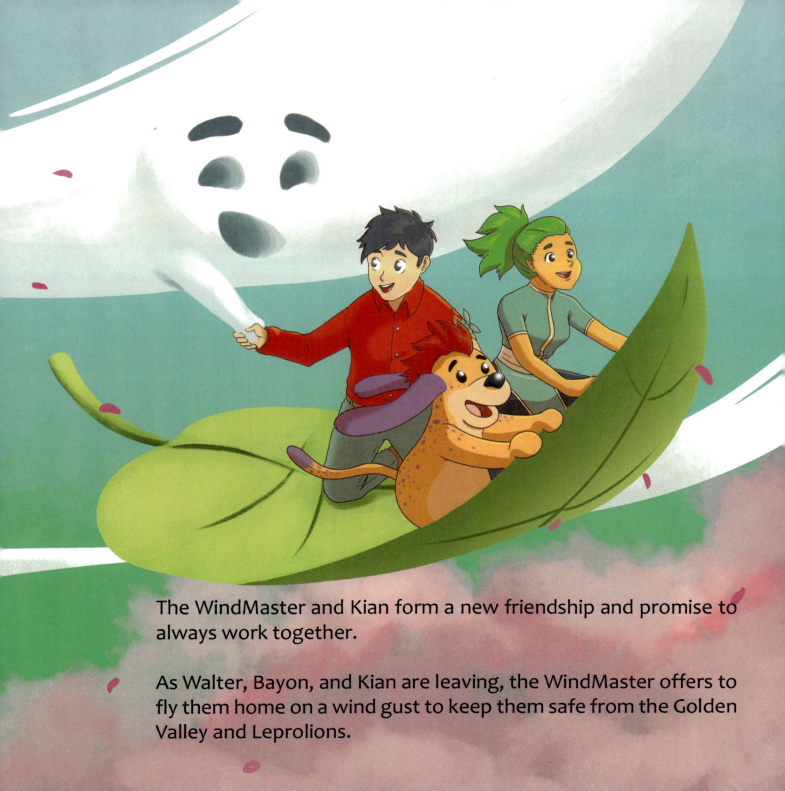

The WindMaster and Kian form a new friendship and promise to always work together.

As Walter, Bayon, and Kian are leaving, the WindMaster offers to fly them home on a wind gust to keep them safe from the Golden Valley and Leprolions.

The village rejoices with the news of the new friendship with the Windpeople. They make a celebration and thank Walter and Bayon, as it would not have been possible without them.

Walter and Bayon are filled with happiness to have helped protect the village and made new friends. After the celebration, it is time to head home to Arizona.

They say goodbye to Kian and walk to the meadow where they find the Vortex.

Walter smiles and pushes the buttons. "I hope it works!" They continue walking, and the next thing they know, they are home!

Made in the USA
Las Vegas, NV
09 March 2024